HOMECOMING

HEATHER BEAMISH

keep it bright

Homecoming
Written by: Heather Beamish

Published by Voices Publishing
Produced with the support of the City of Toronto through the
Toronto Arts Council.

Front cover design by Kira Tejada (@kiratheoddist)
Copy editing by Casselberry Creative Design

ISBN: 9798351573878

THE VOICES PUBLISHING

TORONTO ARTS COUNCIL

DEDICATION

To my beautiful wife, Faithe, and my Grandmothers who have anchored me.

Faithe, I wouldn't be who I am or where I am without you as my partner. Your faithfulness has made up for all the ways life has disappointed me. Your kindness has swaddled my heart in lavender. Your playful-humor has painted my world with streaks of gold. Your love has held me down, built me up and made me more.

Grandma Beamish, thank you for your wisdom, example and generosity. Your unending support has created a sturdy foundation for me to stand on.

Grandmere Smith, thank you for your songs, prayers and friendship. Your legacy of faith and resilience has nourished generations.

TABLE OF CONTENTS

Hello, my precious reader.

My name is Heather, my pronouns are she/her, and I am so excited that you have chosen to join me on this journey. During our time together, I am going to be combining the captivatingly colourful cadences of poetry with snapshots and reflections from my life. My hope is that my words and stories connect with your heart and infuse your mind with visions of hope and possibility.

For we need to cultivate our hope
because it fuels our struggle
Giving us the vision to see
the potential within the rubble

The past few years of my life have been such a beautiful, uncomfortable, and freeing adventure. Six years ago I stepped away from my full-time job as a pastor in a conservative, evangelical church so that I could explore my queerness without the weight of shame I was living under. I honestly didn't know if it was going to be worth it. I didn't know if I would find what I was looking for.

I was blocked in
Boxed in
Pushed to the bottom
So I grabbed my pen and started shoveling
I didn't see my intersections celebrated on your stages
So I built my own
Took paint and sharpies and drew myself the world I wanted
Now I'm finally home
You refused to give me a hand up
So I wrote my way out
Created doors from your bottom floors

Now we've got an underground rail route

This book is full of discovery and struggle, disappointments and triumph. It's going to take you on a poetic pilgrimage through the moments that inspired personal discoveries and introduce you to the medicines that healed me along the journey. Choosing to stop living for other people and dedicating time to learning how to cherish and treasure myself has made me more resilient. It has invited me into the process of shedding shame, connecting with my body, embracing equitable worldviews, building authentic relationships and finding my voice.

The truth is
I left you and I blossomed
I left you and I soared
Broke through your ceilings
And authored myself a life that I adore

I love intention setting. Before jumping into a new experience or doing something risky, my partner and I like to name what we want and how we are showing up to that moment. It creates space for us to bring our desires and fears into the open so that we can affirm and support each other. It helps us to be more deliberate and live into deeper levels of awareness around what our bodies are communicating to us through our emotions and senses. Writing this book definitely falls under the category of a new and risky experience, so before we jump in, I want to share a few of my intentions with you, my dear reader.

That you would be captivated
by the tasty potential of our collective liberation

My hope is that as you immerse yourself in these poems and pages, you will connect to the wisdom of your emotions in greater degrees. This book is full of affirmations and hopeful imaginings because self-love is healthy. Feeling good in the body and the life you have is generative. So as you read pieces that connect with you, I encourage you to speak them over your own soul. Write them out and make them your own. Lean into the gentle invitation to reflect and embody love as you experience life through the lens of my intersections. May these word-seeds become keys that unlock new dreams and realities for you to live into. May - inspire strides that cause you to rise and see the world through new eyes. May it pave a way for your homecoming.

Pull up a Chair - *A Spoken Word Poem*

Two postures are important
Two postures are where we need to begin
One, requires courageous honesty
The other, a softness to let those words sink in
Two sides of the coin exist
Two sides need to be explored
One, the dominant narrative
The other, marginalized stories that can no longer be ignored

Today, I am asking you to
Come and listen
Come and let the forgotten one feel heard
Clothe your siblings with the dignifying garments
Of hanging off of their every word
Heard and held
Held and healed
These steps are simple but if walked out, great will be their
yield

Pull up a chair
And travel a mile in your sister's moccasin
Enter into these narratives
And let your shoulders feel the weight of your brother's oppression
Because sometimes our stories
Are all that we have left
When dreams have been choked out, communities ravaged
And everything in our world
Bears the markings of theft
We must always remember
That compassion is free but healing wounds takes time
So open wide your heart
And allow the power of our stories to birth something divine

CHAPTER ONE

A POETIC LAND ACKNOWLEDGEMENT

Poems about Mother Earth

This book has been written in various fields and forests all over Turtle Island. Hours have been spent lounging and creating in the sun as I penned out poetic imaginings of the future and re-makings of my past. I have been held and healed as the land and I co-created space for reflection and resurrection. To not acknowledge the part she has played in the birthing of this book would be like celebrating the beauty of a tree while ignoring the roots that nourished and supported her thriving. So I want to pause and thank the land for her beauty and medicine. For her earthly wisdom and her chaotic order. She has been present and available through every valley and victory I have experienced. She is dependable and wise. Miigwetch, Mother Earth.

She helps me slow down

When the beautiful invitation came to start working on this book, it was during the initial Covid-19 lockdown and all the spaces I would typically go to write were closed. No libraries, cafés, or co-working spaces were open, and after eight hours of working my day job inside a little condo, I needed a change of scenery to help ward off the cabin fever. So I started walking. I can proudly say that this book has been crafted and created on park benches and picnic tables all over my beautiful city. But the most significant walk happened the day my exploring took me down to the Toronto lakeshore. As I slowed down and took in the rhythmic rippling of the water, my mind finally connected her presence with a collection of healing memories stored in my body. I began to realize how the water's nearness calmed my anxiety - how at ease I was in her presence. She gave me the gift of crisp, fresh air and nourished my cells as her moisture seeped into my pores. She made me feel like all things were possible and I realized how much easier it was to write with her at my side, with her as my muse. As I sat at her feet, she hummed a melody that had a beautiful way of making me want to lean into the vulnerable parts of myself.

She gives me peace

During a week-long writing retreat I took at the Five Oaks campground in Paris, Ontario, I had another significant exchange with the land. The property is surrounded by a vibrant forest and sits at the confluence of two waterways. This wild converging of the powerful and life-giving element of water is revered as holy ground for many Indigenous communities across Turtle Island. So every morning before jumping into writing, I would perch under the sturdy arms of mother Elm and listen. I would soak in the countless stories that rippled along her surface - tales of all the communities she has birthed, cleansed, and nourished.

Going outside helps me go inside

I have found a rich harvest of wisdom and wealth as I have started embracing stillness and taken the time to witness her wild. Spending time in nature has supported reciprocities flourishing and awakened me to the dance of life that is happening all around. As I have practiced honing my ears to the voice of Mother Earth oozing from everything on this planet, my connection with all that is living has been strengthened. Through these channels of relationship, she awakens my soul and invites me to spend differently, rest differently, and live differently. I am learning how to become her friend and protector, and in exchange she gives me the gift of her potent medicines that heal my traumas and mis-regulations. And since our flourishing is interconnected, we both benefit when the exchange is mutual.

My body knows these trees
Generations of rock and soil
Course through the rich streams of my blood
I am of her
And her I
We are one
My body opens up
As she slowly remembers how these branches have held
Centuries of community gatherings

For the land is the best host
She is my daily bread
Sustaining, supporting and satisfying us all
I tilt my head back in joyful abandon
A grateful response to the generous nourishment
She has laid before me

Every time I let my limbs lead the way
Her gravitational pull awakens my inner compass
And I am once again standing at her feet

Meaningless preoccupations wash away
As her nearness captivates my senses
Leaving me both satisfied and wanting

Her eyes are like mirrors glittering with belonging and kinship
I feel seen as she lovingly caresses my body
I pour out my worship as her wisdom dances all around me

My spirit climaxes into peace as I am regulated
By the water

- *Co-Regulation*

Come and be with me
I want to *o v e r w h e l m* your senses
With my effortless seduction
I am vibrant and fierce
Wild yet refined
I am full of endless mystery
Sit with me and let me consume you
You haven't known the true strength of addiction
Until you have plunged into my depths

- Love Letters From Mother Earth

My eyes are glued open
Unwilling to blink for the fear of missing anything
The vibrancy of this moment has arrested all of my senses
I'm transfixed
Pulled under
And in awe

You overwhelm me in all of the right ways

Green grass between my toes
Refreshing scents rising to my nose
This is the good life, I think that's how the story goes
I would like to suggest to you, may I propose
That the most beautiful sight I've seen today was a singular rose
Armani has nothing on that flower's clothes
She doesn't need to flaunt her beauty, because true beauty shows
Swaying softly in the breeze as it blows
Revealing the wonder of her maker
To anyone who would slow down and notice the rose

There is a reason why all of the dreamers
Always have their heads in the clouds
Just look up
I promise it will take your *breath away*

When I look at you
I see endless possibilities
A crisp blank page
I see new horizons ripping through the darkness of my night
You are both mystery and promise
Both hidden and unable to be concealed
You embody moody brilliance perfectly

- Moon

The thickness of their gray
Reminds me that it's okay
To be heavy and emotional

They openly whirl past
In their dark moody mass
Reminding me it's okay to cry

-Clouds

Have you ever considered how much the Earth needs our breath
How much she needs our deep-bellied exhales
Dripping with condensation
How we have been designed to be interdependent
Health flourishing in our exchange of particles
Have you ever watched
How our breath naturally reaches for the
Sky as we let it go

Pillowing clouds replenished as we give her our guttural sighs
The same chi that detoxifies us as we forcefully exhale
Is received as a gift that nourishes her
Doesn't that image reek of her wisdom and reciprocity

-Breath

Earth, wind, fire, and water
Her might and mystery draws me
Lands and lakes
Her curves and quakes
It's her glory that captivates and awes me

Ashes to ashes and dust to dust
Our Mother holds us in our most vulnerable states
So let's shower her with love and care
On this earth day, also known as her birthday
And let the future enjoy the world we co-create

- *Earth Day*

CHAPTER TWO

THE GIFT OF WRITING

Poems about Art

I used to live a very noisy life. I would have a calendar packed full of commitments and activities that kept me occupied from morning to night. I justified my exhausting schedule by telling myself that this was simply the life of an extrovert. But as I have made space for reflection and healing, I discovered my addiction to noise and chaos was birthed out of an avoidance coping mechanism. If I never slowed down and let the external world get quiet, I would not have to confront my numbness, unpack my traumas, or feel my disappointment.

A quiet space

After giving so much of my energy, time and attention to the busy world that exists outside of myself, a beautiful invitation in the form of a writing deadline came along and carved out a quiet space for reflection and creation. Writing this book has pushed me to limit the number of extra commitments I can have. It has given me the opportunity to create a magical space where can tenderly examine the events of my life. It has asked me to curiously reflect on my intersectional journey into self-discovery and liberation. And because it's a book of poetry, it has given me the healing container of art to pour my countless racing thoughts into.

A magical space

Writing poetry has never been about throwing flowery words onto paper. Poetry requires the participation of your heart. It is thoughtful and asks you to be particular about each word that is selected to ensure it embodies the right emotion. As a result, this project has asked me to carefully feel into my life's happenings. I've had time to cry out bitter toxins and release painful memories as my heart has been validated by the gentle strokes of my keyboard. I'm noticing that the chaos and clammer that used to characterize my cluttered inner world is being replaced with a gentle acceptance of what is, and a hopeful expectation of what will be. Artful reflection has made room for me to experiment and explore my intersections without my inner critic ambushing me with shame and fear. I am healing up and learning how to cultivate an energetic atmosphere that is allowing my roots to breathe and my branches to shimmer.

I tend to process my feelings and capture milestones
Through words written
Letting letters and sounds ooze out of me
Like a fruit bitten
Although my default is to keep these fragile pieces protected
Under lock and key
Safely tucked away from the harm of
Others' scrutiny
I have felt this gentle invitation
Calling me into the open
To share candidly about life, pain, love
And who I put my hope in
So here I am committing to simply show up
In my own skin
Knowing that as I come out
There is room for you to come in

This is a work of passion
So I shamelessly take my time unwrapping you
I allow my body to thrum with pleasure as I
S
L
O
W
L
Y
And methodically peel back every inch of your mystery
I tenderly lay my precious pearls at your feet
Flushed as you respond with meticulous wanting

-*The Writing Process*

Writing invites the
M o v e m e n t
Of emotions
So I pick up my pen and
S u r r e n d e r
To the current
Of her oceans
My pen keeps me rooted
So I nurture our *connection*
Shedding off old skins
As she brings me to *resurrection*

Art has always been
my avenue for processing feelings
and calling out the *system*

Both outlets needed
for healing and a fresh perspective
for those who *listen*

My detox happens
Every time pen hits paper
Sweating out feelings like toxins
And letting them dissipate like vapor
Reflect and release
Then acknowledge and feel
With each step forward I gradually heal

Sometimes the build-up of emotions is so real
Pen and paper always knowing how to draw out
What I really feel
Helping me digest
Helping me deal
Helping me organize my thoughts and exposing roots
That I ignore and conceal

Non-judgmental and always curious
Patient and ready to take me serious
Thank you words
Thank you art
Thank you universe
Thank you from the bottom of my heart

Write the vision and make it plain
Detailing the steps and calling them by name
See yourself possessing, achieving, owning, being
Replay that track until you have what you are seeing
Write a story that you are excited to call yours
Then get up and have it as the universe opens up doors

Birthed in the slimy recesses
of your cranial cave
The idea seemed foolish
but your passion made you brave
You pushed past the naysayers
and those who were determined to limit you
Excited to exceed the expectations
of those that you once knew
You relished the risk and adventure
found in forging a path that was yours alone
Authoring a life that wasn't cookie-cutter
or a factory-made clone

I write for my healing

I wrestle words down until they are in full submission; penned
I fearlessly conjure up feelings that have been assigned to
haunt
And without blinking I capture their deformed details with coal

I heal from my writing

CHAPTER THREE

TEMPLE WORSHIP

Poems about the Body

I was always an awkward-looking kid. Raised by my single dad and surrounded by three brothers, I was your textbook tomboy. However, as I grew older, the differences between my siblings and me became more prominent. I remember taking a bath in middle school and vigorously scrubbing my legs because I had noticed black specks of dirt all over them. When the black dots failed to disappear, I realized with dismay that it wasn't dirt but my newly grown leg hair. In fact, when I bled for the first time, it was my childhood best friend, Brittany, who had her mom bring me pads and explain my period to me. The gawkiness of puberty had struck but I had no one to talk to about everything that was happening in my body.

I doubted your capacity

Wary of the continuous developments in my body, I decided that the best solution was to ignore them altogether. Distraction and avoidance became my default response to any and all overwhelming feelings my body tried to communicate. In high school, I became involved in a conservative Christian community that espoused the idea that your body was solely meant to be used to honour god. These teachings taught me to shame and repress the same-sex attractions I was feeling. This repression, paired with the patriarchal standards of servitude and oppressive gender roles that society clamped around my neck as a woman, left me feeling even more confused and confined in my body. This resulted in years of silencing my body's involvement in vital conversations about protection and pleasure and capped her contribution to that of a servant, instead of a collaborator.

I release every voice that speaks to me from the place of woundedness

In so many ways I had become the walking dead. I was here, but not fully. Disconnected from my body, I smothered her voice and caged her cravings so she wouldn't take me down a path of destruction. Learning about the tenets of critical feminism and liberation theology through the writings of Bell Hooks and James Cone began to re-wire my thinking and open my mind. Their writing encouraged me to question the scripts I had been handed and confront systems of power that worked to exclude and marginalize my existence. I started feeling empowered to use my voice to advocate for my body and approach her as my wise and respected partner. These truths became the scalpel I used to extract harmful cancers from my belief system and clear the dam that was clogging my access to her voice.

Believe the voice that calls you beautiful

Pushing against narratives of shame and surrounding myself with open-minded, powerful humans has been vital in unlocking the ancient library of knowledge and creativity coded within the fabric of my melanated curves. Unshackling my mind from oppressive conditioning and inviting the untamed desires of my body to roam freely has been messy and exhilarating. It has given me the chance to practice giving my body permission to explore the full spectrum of her capacities and not shy away from the intensity of her desires. Plunging into the depths of those energetic forces has allowed me to embody a higher-quality existence. Learning to prioritize pleasure, respect, affinity, and exploration has cleared a space for her to be heard and seen, showing me that on the other side of repression is the sweet gift of expression.

Dear Body,

I trust you
I trust that you instinctively know how to nurture
And protect
And care for me
Because you always have

I see how you pulled from your deep reserves
Of ancestral resilience
And evolved
And triumphed
Your observant knowings lead me like a compass
And I am enjoying our adventure

Affectionately yours,

- *Consciousness*

I am the priest of this body
I am the keeper of this blessing

My energy and attitude answer to me
Both are under my jurisdictional authority
So I declare peace
I claim my inheritance of joy
I ask for wisdom and divine inspiration
I cultivate these seeds with luminescent visualizations

I am the priest of this house
I am the keeper of this temple

For so long I was scared of touch
Thought if I asked for it
I'd be seen as creepy or too much
So I deprived my body and silenced the ache
I cultivated my mind
While detaching limbs to dissociate
But my skin screams for nearness from you
Throbbing for connection and contact

Teach me how to let you hold me

These days
I choose to hold and caress her tenderly
I pause more to notice and relish her gentle intakes of breath
I try not to dismiss her subtle prompts about
My safety, joy and energy
These days
I am giving my body the space she deserves

I am at a party
And my body is touched
And slapped
And fought over
And stared at
And used as currency
And scrutinized
And ignored
And coveted
And all it really wants
Is to be seen and savored

Cosmic wonder
Caged in human skin
Your eyes the gateway
Your soul my portal in

You tell me how much I am allowed to feed my body
Nourished but always left wanting
You dictate the clothes I am allowed to drape over my limbs
An extensive rule book exists outlining
Who I can look at, engage with and be touched by
Rules that leave me feeling small, suffocated and unseen

Today I break the silence and let her speak

Slow down and let your breath guide you home
Live in your body again
Love in your body again
Cocoon your daily dealings in kindness
Own and elevate the atmosphere all around you

I am youthful and radiant
Because that is the atmosphere I cultivate

I am liberated and empowered
Because those are the truths that daily permeate

I'm talking,
Best days are on the way
I've got ancestral wisdom coursing through my veins
Kind of attitude

Palms sweating
Mind forgetting
Tongue not letting
Fear

Shoulders pushed high
Chest unable to sigh
Heart thundering like the sky
Stress

Hands grabbing skin
Lips locking in
Passion piloting
Lust

CHAPTER FOUR

AN ACCESSIBLE GOSPEL

Poems about God

M y relationship with God was a "love at first sight" kind of story. When my parents divorced, my mom moved to the Toronto suburb of Brampton where she got very connected to a Pentecostal Christian community. Every other weekend when my brother and I visited her we would spend two of the three days at church singing mantras of empowerment and hearing sermons about the love of God. I was introduced to a kind creator who loved me and had prosperous plans for my life. I learned how to let go of worry and fear and lean on a friend that would walk with me through every valley and fire.

God and I go way back

This chapter is particularly important because I feel like it's my chance to give a character reference for someone that means a lot to me. She has been a kind and loyal friend even when there was nothing for her to gain from our relationship. Those low and lonely periods linger in my mind because they tell me everything I need to know about what she is like, about her character. But the name of God is being used by religion to foster division and sanction discrimination and as someone who has tasted and seen that she is good, I feel compelled to be

55

her witness.

Today, God told me
She missed my prayers

When I left the church to explore my sexuality, I stopped reading my Bible and going to church. After a lifetime of hearing that God hated my gay, I internalized those words and started to believe what they told me. But even when our relationship was strained, God was relentless in showering me with her care and kindness. I was reminded of a God who goes out of her way to let every person, from every background and walk of life, know that they matter. In the Gospels, the religious authorities of the time shunned and shamed the people Jesus chose to be in his inner circle. They appointed themselves the gatekeepers to the divine and made difficult and arbitrary qualifications for membership. Then Jesus came and broke down the barriers of exclusion and lavished interest on those overlooked by society. He established spacious avenues of access to God and lived out a gospel of love.

Vision matters
How we see ourselves, the world, and the future
Matters

Publicly taking up space as a queer Christian has brought visibility to our existence and helped me reclaim access to my spiritual inheritance. But this time I am integrating the wealth of wisdom I have gleaned from both communities. The queer community has taught me that transformational power is unlocked when we approach life with the posture of curiosity and celebration. They have shown me that critiquing and deconstructing institutions that are harmful can be a beautiful invitation into growth and healing. It has highlighted the importance of affirming religious spaces that promote inclusivity and embody love for all of God's family, no exceptions. Spaces that reflect those values publicly in their policy, practices, and promotion - because faith without deeds is dead. I have seen that when the vision is spacious and the practices are generative, the individual and the community flourish.

God is beautiful and expansive
Her kindness and generosity confound our carnal and
calculating minds

These days, my relationship with higher-power is less prescriptive and more expansive. I have learned the value of approaching the divine with a reverent curiosity. This posture has opened up new avenues for seeing God's beauty beyond the steeple. It has opened my heart to cherish how other religions and cultures have cultivated communion with the Divine over the centuries. It has challenged me to find ways to build bigger tables of inclusion and access to God.

Everyday New - *A Spoken Word Poem*

Jesus surrendered his privilege and power
To elevate marginalized voices
He was counter-cultural and subversive
With each and every one of his choices
He came to earth and embodied
How perfect love would interact with my humanity
His commitment to love and inclusion
Highlighted the core essentials for Christianity
He was courageously vulnerable
Nurturing and bold
He spoke truth to power and accepted everyone into his fold
Messy people never made him uncomfortable or nervous
He stood up for what he cared for; it was never just lip-service

This is why I have chosen to let my guard down
And lean into a power that makes all things new
This is why I won't walk away from a God
Who enters into my darkness to guide me through
These seeds of fire
This resilient life that won't be aborted
Each decision to keep showing up
My community that keeps me supported
New
Everyday, we are being made new

We will follow the way of love
Letting her tender nudges guide us
We will follow the way of love
Letting her persistent presence heal us
Drape our eyes with filters of compassion
Consume our hearts with visions of hope

May our hands stay soft and reaching
And our mouths be fountains of healing
May our desire be our prayer
And our work bring about its manifestation
May our visions be filled with fields of possibility
And our faithfulness bring about their harvest
Because that's when judgement and fear depart
Because that's when liberation and transformation start

Above all, we ask for wisdom
Before all, we seek understanding
We will follow the way of love
And stay loyal to what love is commanding

– *Our Community Posture*

I am a witness
To life
To hope
To resurrection
A violent uprising against death
I am the insurrection
I am the voice of truth
Resounding through our barren lands
An invitation brimming with potential
As each word-seed is scattered by my hands
I've been sent to remind you
That the promise has come and the kingdom is near
Sent to spur to action
All of those who would have ears to hear

I am your friend
I am the lion and the shooting star
My love is near
Following you even when my hands feel far
I am the signal and the sign
My wonders twinkle around your hemisphere
I am the carnal and the divine
Harmoniously reminding you that my love is here

My friends say that I am a dreamer
And I own that title with pride
Because I know the breeding ground for miracles
Is when vision and faith collide

Look again
Your promise rolls in on a cloud
I see her in the distance
Look again
Your breakthrough is in the room
It's the fruit of your persistence
I said, look again
Dawn is breaking
And her light is cascading and clarifying and calling
Look again
Thirsty lands are being quenched and renewal rains are falling
Look again
I said look again

The religious people didn't want me in the room
In their minds they had me labelled and all figured out
But the problem is
They have always underestimated me
Cast me away and confined me
They were focused on all the wrong things
Position, power, prominence
But I ignored their criticisms
And kept my eyes fixed on the person
Who made all of the risk worth it
I knew he was going to see the real me
I knew I wouldn't be left hanging

My love was not meant to be commodified
Or turned into a membership program
It's expansive, inclusive and eternally free

- *God*

Against all hope, we, in hope, believe
Being fully persuaded that what God promised
She has the power to let us receive

– Romans 4:18 Remixed

Fresh start
New heart
Lord, you called me out from my grave
I was used up
Bruised up
And no longer able to be brave

Like a cynic I overlooked you
Jaded from loss and lies, I fought you
But still, you tenderly called
How did I get so lucky to have such a patient creator
Your ways, much higher than mine
Your heart, more open than mine
Your love is a scandal
Your grace my mind can barely handle
Your love is straight scandalous!

Institutions do not have exclusive rights to accessing God
She is all over
All around
And inside us

Holy, high, heavenly, and haunted
Where attendance is necessary and devotion is wanted
Each week patrons reverently file into their pews
Letting the words of the Bible shape their worldviews

Haunted, heavenly, holy and high
Where power isn't questioned and members turn a blind eye
To discrimination, manipulation and inappropriate behaviour
Stealing from the poor while claiming Jesus as their saviour

High, holy, haunted and heavenly
I painted my face and hid my shadows cleverly
Singing all the songs and reciting the right lines
Heart not invested, they should have seen the signs

Heavenly, haunted, high and holy
The church is growing but it is doing so too slowly
I wanted to belong but could no longer believe
The hungry skeptic in me kept nudging me to leave

I finally learnt that I could have those things on my own
Heavenly encounters over day-old coffee
Holy perfection staring back at me in the dark
Haunted moments void of consequence
High

Why do we need to keep on dreaming?

Because we matter
Because our future matters
Because our systems are oppressive and extractive and
dangerous and they need to be exposed
Because our present ways of living are not sustainable or
equitable to both humanity and the beautiful planet that gives
us life
Because information doesn't move us like art does
Because we need our hearts connected to intellectual and
intangible realities
Because art connects our hearts to intellectual and intangible
realities

CHAPTER FIVE

THE TABLE

A Poem about Coming Out

Announcing your sexuality to the world is not a necessary rite of passage for all queer folks. It can be a liberating declaration that breaks down bar-ers of duplicity and it can be a label that makes you a target of discrimination. Coming out can be a significant part of living into your sexuality and gender identity, but disclosure should always be a decision that is made by the individual. Unfortunately, I was outed by people from my former religious community. In their mouths, my sexuality journey was coloured with a judgment and shame that I had outgrown. I needed to take my power back and reclaim my narrative so I shared the below coming out post on social media.

Facebook Post - April 2017
A year ago I decided to embark on one of the scariest adventures of my life - a journey of self-discovery that has become one of the most stressful, nail-biting, exciting and liberating seasons. It began when I quit my full-time job as a pastor, broke up with my boyfriend of 2.5 years and moved to a whole new city. Once settled, I also began to "unpack" what was going on in my heart and life, which has led to some beautiful, but costly, outcomes.

My church took a firm stance of rejection, part of my family resisted the news, friendships that I have had since childhood dissolved, and my faith was shaken. However, I can honestly say that a year and a half later, I am in a healthier place now than I was before. I have found a great faith community, been loved on by so many people, deconstructed/reconstructing my faith, thrown off layers of shame and finally fallen in love with myself.

In an effort to come out to a lot of people at once (because coming out can be emotionally exhausting and is sometimes annoying to have to do over and over again) AND to reclaim my story from those who would maliciously gossip about me behind my back (you know who you are - and SURPRISE! So do I), I have written this post. All of the reactions listed below are real situations that have happened to me. In sharing them, I hope to help you understand what some of this journey has been like for me. Enjoy!

5. *"Don't worry, we can fix this."* - My Old Counsellor

After I told my old pastor/boss that I was wrestling with these same-sex feelings and that I might be gay, she proceeded to set me up with mandatory counselling sessions. In our first session, my right-wing, conservative Christian counsellor started out by telling me that my boss had told him what "the issue" was and that he was the right man for the job of fixing me. He continued to tell me that he had seen situations like this in the past and that if I was willing to confess my sinful desires and surrender to the will of God, we could have things back to normal in no time.

After many months of going to these sessions, I decided that although I am imperfect and value the expertise of the counselling profession, I was not broken in the area of my sexual orientation.

4. *"I never pegged you as 'The gay type'"* - **One of my friends from high school**

What the heck does that even mean? Lol.

So, I know my friend. She is a kind-hearted, open-minded person who didn't mean to sound ignorant in her response but was obviously caught off guard and so that kind of just came out. I think her response shines a light on the fact that there are a lot of stereotypes surrounding the queer community and that keeping an open mind is so important when supporting loved ones.

I have found that being ME, and not who or what others think I should be, has been so healthy and liberating.

3. *"Are you sure you're not Bi?"* - **Guy that was trying to date me**

As I was preparing myself for all the different reactions that people would have to me telling them that I was gay, this one never even crossed my mind. I had rehearsed scenarios of joy, shock, disapproval or support, but never this one.

There I was, sitting in a restaurant trying to explain to this man why his desire to have a romantic relationship with me would never actualize. In past conversations, I had told him that "I wasn't ready" or that "it was me and not him," but this time I had worked up the courage to be honest with him. So, I took a deep breath and blurted out, "I'm gay!" I slowly looked up, expecting there to be signs of revelation and understanding. Instead, after a long pause, he said, "Are you sure you're not Bi?"

2. *"But how can you be gay and a Christian?"* - **Church**

friend
This singular question is what has kept me up countless nights. It is what kept me in the closet for so many years. It is what pushed me to read countless books on the subject, spill my messy story to complete strangers and ask myself some of the rawest and most difficult questions ever.

I definitely don't have all of the answers when it comes to faith and sexuality but I am firmly rooted in the belief that God has created, loves and enjoys all people. And to expound upon Paul's words in Romans 8:

For I am convinced that neither death nor life, neither angels nor demons, neither the present nor the future, nor any powers, neither height nor depth, neither sexual orientation nor gender identity, nor anything else in all creation will be able to separate us from the love of God that is in Christ Jesus our Lord.

1. *"Honey, it's okay, I'm a lesbian, too."* - My Dad
This was my Dad's attempt to calm my nerves in his classic "Dad-Humor" style and let me know that he was okay with my news. My dad, brothers and a handful of close friends have been my rock during this time. I am forever thankful for your love and kindness, because in the words of Amy Poehler, "It's easier to be brave when you're not alone."

Well if you didn't know, now you know.

- Heather

As soon as I hit "post" on the above text, I closed my computer and leaned into the moral support of the people that I was with. Hours later, I checked back and my post, feed and inbox were flooded with comments and messages from people from the different seasons of my life. Initially, lots of kind words were shared but as time passed, I started to get cutting emails and text messages. People that haven't spoken to me in months, even years, felt it was their religious duty to warn me of the impending hellfires that awaited me if I continued on this path of "gayness." So, the below piece was birthed out of all the feelings that I had to sift through.

The Table – *A Spoken Word Poem*

I'm trying
I'm trying to let the love be
Louder than all this hate
But it's hard to stand tall
When with their words they emasculate
They denigrate
They try to negate
My place at Your table
My place in this pew
My place in the front-lines
Doing ministry for You
They say,
"Well, I'm told to hate the sin and love the sinner"
But with their actions
They cheapen their words and make them thinner
They say,
"Go back into the closet and lose the key,"
With each careless slur
Throwing further judgment on me

But I say to them
It's not your table
You don't have the right to block my way
It's not your table
You can't keep me out, just because I'm gay
It's not your table
You won't have the final say because
It's.
Not.
Your.
Table.

After I've taken the time
To vent and feel
And I've allowed the defences
Of my heart to unsteel
In stillness and reflection
I find Your peace
Allowing me to let go of the control
And just cease
Cease striving
And defending
And trying to prove that I belong
Cease performing
And cowering
And dancing along to their song
Because Your invitation
Has been extended to me
All along

For you prepare a table before me
In the presence of my enemies
You anoint my head with oil
My cup overflows
Surely Your goodness and mercy
Will follow me all the days of my life
And I will dwell in the house of the Lord
Forever!

CHAPTER SIX

ACTIVISM

Poems about Race + Intersectionality

As a queer woman of colour that grew up in primarily white, straight spaces, I am very familiar with the ways this world works to control and confine my uniqueness through the crushing tentacles of oppression. Learning how to love and embrace my intersectionality has been a lifelong journey. Growing up in the countryside where my family was one of the only families of colour, my Jamaican, Irish and Indigenous roots left me feeling othered as I struggled to find belonging. My hair, which stood atop my head defying gravity with each kinky coil, always gave me away as being different. Instead of embracing each curly strand, I used every product I could find to straighten and tame my hair with the goal of emulating all my white friends. It wasn't until I moved to Brampton and was surrounded by diversity that I began to see the beauty in my hair and even later in life, that I truly believed it.

I descend from a long line of warriors

As an adult, I have realized that my lineage is ripe with stories of systemic oppression and resistance. The complexity of experiencing the world as a mixed-race queer woman has taught me to both embrace my labels and understand that I am more than my labels. However, this duality is not mirrored in the way society views me and navigating the world with this understanding can be overwhelming. Racism causes people to approach my beautiful melanated curves with fear. Homophobia taints the radiant love I share with my same-sex partner and calls it a perversion. Misogyny undervalues my voice, contribution, and capacity based on my clothes and body parts.

Don't forget who you are

For so long I had a very limited vocabulary for the inequities that I experienced and didn't yet know how to use my voice to express or protect myself. Advocating for myself and the communities I am part of started when I began building diverse groups of belonging. As I became exposed to conversations and content that was naming the broken systems my marginalized identities had to navigate, I began to feel validated and empowered. The solidarity and resonance I found in community gave me the courage to start demanding that individuals and institutions learn how to treat us with the dignity and respect we deserve. My chosen family reminded me that I am worth fighting for, and self-education gave me the language to advocate for that change.

You are the love-child of Mother Earth's most beautiful fantasies

Spoken word poetry has become my instrument of choice for challenging traditional narratives and bringing about positive change. Living in a time when information is everywhere, I believe that art is needed to support communal healing because its main goal is to cause the listener/reader to feel something. Transformation happens when truth is embodied, not just intellectualized. We need the singers, dancers, poets, and feelers to all use their unique voices to humanize differences and bring about change. There is nothing more satisfying than using your craft to expand people's hearts and minds to dream of a more inclusive, equitable and vibrant world.

Art has always been my outlet
For processing feelings and calling out the system
Both avenues needed for healing
And a fresh perspective for those who listen

The swirling difference of my heritage puzzles you
You stare at my hair, my fair skin and try to analyze my accent
for some hint of lineage
But what your peering gaze fails to detect is the fusion of
worlds that pumps through my veins
You see, I am the product of nations colliding
Not a half-breed, but fully bred as a creation of intersecting
wonder
These lines are both coloured-in with care and leaving just the
right amount of white space for my uniqueness to be
accentuated
So next time you come up to me and ask, "What are you?!"
You will understand why I pause
Before trying to summarize my mystery

Who do you turn to for help
When the institutions that are meant to protect you have failed
Whose court do you appeal to
When the corruption of your government is the reason you're
jailed
Lofty dreams are promised but only crumbs are plated
Appetites wet with longing
But hindered by a structure that was designed to keep your life
deflated

I want change
This hate is outdated
We demand change
So many deserve to be exonerated
This must change
Brick by brick until this colonial system is obliterated

So you're telling me
That you're offended by my insistence that "Black Lives Matter"
Feeling that my language is divisive,
And a little too aggressive, and that I should really be more inclusive
But you're not offended by how this country treats black bodies
Beats black bodies
How it imprisons and cheats black bodies
Leaving us to die in the streets, black bodies
Is this really the kind of society that your vision of unity embodies?

Let's look at the facts and agree that the scales haven't been
evenly cast
Recognizing we're all needed to create change and break the
violent cycle of our past
And although words are important, talk alone is not enough
True integrity looks like living into our values even when the
decisions are tough
It looks like paying attention to the wisdom and experience
coming from marginalized voices
Understanding that how we spend our money, our friendships
and hiring practices are all politically charged choices
So let's find ways to share privilege, advocate for equality, and
increase representation
Show up for marches, take time to really listen, and help
shoulder the burden of education
Because being part of the change is simple but it also comes
with a cost
But our payment will be
Our sweat
Our love
Our labour
Our commitment
And n o t another black life lost

I've been looking around the world a lot lately
and I keep on seeing darkness, doom, and despair
I keep on being disappointed by our systems
and the choices of the people who hold the power
I long to see us step into our elevated potential

So, I am training my eyes
to look beyond what they are currently seeing
I am teaching my mind
to focus on what is good, right, pure and lovely in this life
I'm guiding my hands
to shop more consciously and give more generously
I am beginning to speak those ancient blessings over my soul;
Those truths that tell me, that I am not alone
That I do not need to sit in fear or discouragement
because I am supported and held by the universe

Corrupt systems and people steeped in hate
Want to ensure that doors and opportunities are closed
But the harder they push us down
The stronger our resistance grows
Because oppression ultimately breeds the power to oppose

If pessimism fixates on the potential harm
And optimism ignores the blood on our hands
I will choose a perspective
That is rooted in the reality of our damaged present
And a hopeful determination that gives time
To let our *consistent, conscious, choices compound*

5 guys, 5 lives
Buried under piles of contrived lies
Legal system unable to see past their dark skin and blood-ties
Still-birth dreams handed to them like midwives
Their stories expose a system that exploits blacks as it thrives
So we must keep fighting for reform
Until justice wins and hate dies
Until they finally see that our black lives
Matter

- *The Exonerated Five*

Majestic kinky manes
That were designed to grow tall and take up lots of space
Naturally mirroring
The prophetic appearing
Of what oppressors were fearing
For this brilliant, resilient race

I sit on panels
And feel excluded from conversations
I've experienced

Simplicity is the language of access

I sit here thinking about my heritage
Ready to engage
Scanning my memories for moments of connectedness
That I could bring to center stage
But as I review my childhood narratives
I see assimilation on every page
Being encouraged to explore my white interests
And told my black ones to cage
Straighten your hair
Pull up your pants
Turn off that reggae
Don't move like that when you dance
Enunciate your words
Don't hang with that crowd
Marry a white man
It will make your family proud

Awareness is growing and more acknowledgements are being made
But tokenizing lip service is not sufficient for the damage that needs to be paid
Until missing and killed indigenous women are a national priority
And our nation acknowledges its genocide and stops undermining native authority
Until the bi-products of bigotry and colonization are owned and addressed
And stolen land is returned and indigenous communities have a place to rest
We must be committed to listening better, seeing better, sharing better, doing better

Is it my crown that makes you jealous?
Authority and rule eloquently shaping my jaw
Each shimmering jewel punctuating a lineage teeming with
promise
I implore you not to covet
This is simply
My inheritance

CHAPTER SEVEN

MEDICINES THAT HEALED ME

Poems about Therapy + Self-Help

I can remember look ng at the landscape of my relationships and inner wcrld and longing for more. I wanted to have authentic, reciprocal life-giving connections but kept on being derailed by the cycles of trauma I saw myself repeating. Until I was introduced to the rich library of tools in the self-help and somatic therapy fielcs.

Knowing the type of person you want to be
And being the type of person you want to know,
Are two very different realities.

During thercpy my human longing to be seen was quenched as my therapist validated the survival techniques I developed to claw a space out for myself in my childhood. As those memories were held, I was freed up to heal because I no longer needed to preserve their existence. Reflection, gratitude, and meditation continue to be avenues I use to sharpen my critical thinking, allowing me to harness the creative potential of my mind. Pairing those intellectual tools with the embodied practices of yoga, exercise, somatic therapy and rest, has allowed me to concoct a custom salve that is healing the traumas embedded in the deep tissues of my being.

I will not be passive
About any habit
That steals life's juicy nourishment

The biggest gift of these practices is the way they have created a space for my body, heart, and mind to be centered and their well-being prioritized. They have given me the skills to confront and nullify generational curses that have haunted my lineage. Encased in their wisdom, I watch myself transform. Surrendered to their authority, blossoms of peace, patience, and kindness color my countenance and I attract life-giving connections that vibrate on the same frequency.

I will silence
the voices of
pride and scarcity

So I've made a commitment to never again be passive in the face of any habit that steals even a drop of life's juicy nourishment from me. I will continue to prioritize the prospering of this temple because this is my home and I am worth the investment. I will not let the voices of lack or ego hold me back from accessing professional help when I struggle to actualize those changes on my own. I will remember that some fixes are surface-level and quick, while others require deep excavation and are messy. Whatever the undertaking, I will take it one day at a time because I have everything I need to live an abundant life.

I reject your poison
I see through your sorcery
I cancel your darkness with each deliberate step forward
With my growth
I will continue to evolve form and shed skins
Until the bulging boxes you put me in
B U R S T

Peace around you
Starts with peace within you
Letting life and truth grow
From the spaces that have been you
Developing yourself
Nurturing inner health
Making room for your heart
To breathe

Giving up is easy
All you have to do is roll over and stop caring

Giving up is comfortable
You can't fai if you're never daring

Giving up is common
Commitment and passion are an unusual pairing

Giving up is costly
It will drain you of your confidence and leave you despairing

Giving up is tempting
But please don't give up

What if you turned off your phone, Netflix and all other
distractions
Stilled your mind and listened to your heart's whispering
reactions
Making room for direction, refreshing and inner peace
All of this is possible when you become still and learn to release

I've always had to be the strong one
Had to be the reliable one
Shoulders cemented into sturdy pillars
Energy spent on serving
And caring
And fixing
And showing up for everyone, except for myself

But I am learning how to create space for my roots to reach
and breathe
Learning how to value my softness
Allowing my heart to be both resilient and open
Allowing my body to be both alert and carefree
Allowing my mind to be both engaged and creative
Allowing my entire being to drink of my soul's deep wells of
wisdom and emotion
This is where my strength comes from

Like a water tower that is always pumping, *I pour*
Nourishing vineyards, quenching urges but there is always need
for more

Like a lighthouse that is always flashing, *I shine*
Unmoving through storms, burning bright in blackness but never
able to be just mine

But I am neither a tower nor a building
And my bones are worn down from years of hoisting you up
So I step back and care for myself

I shed you like dry skin
Effortlessly
Painlessly
Permanently

Practice makes perfect
Unless what you've been taught to practice
Is problematic
Resulting in perfectly practiced patterns
That persistently peck away at the
Precious pulsing parts of your heart
Leaving you paralyzed and pillaged

They call me a late bloomer
Insinuating that my years of careful marination were wasted
Implying that the artful ways I allowed my features to emerge
Should have been rushed
They show me their impressive collection of mass-produced
achievements and beam
Glue still wet from haste
Design repeated from copy and paste
But I'm not buying what they are selling
My branches gleam organic
My roots are familiar with the effort required to forge for
nourishment
Struggle shining through my crevices like a stained glass mural
- Brilliant
Skin toughened by years of toil - Resilient
They call me a late bloomer
But I understand the rhythm of the seasons

CLINGING - *A Spoken Word Poem*

Broken connectors got me clinging
I latch onto you when the ache of my heart won't stop ringing
I can feel myself being too much
Too chatty
Too eager
I can feel myself needing your touch
Your attention
Your gaze
I can feel myself, feeling

So instead of facing and dealing
I run
I hide
I bury
I obsess
So instead of confronting and revealing
I numb
I cling
I avoid
I regress
So instead, I just let it all build up in my head
Instead

But,
I've always had this tendency
Needing their approval
I've always hid behind this dependency
Volunteering my own removal
Ever since you left us and didn't come back
My tank developed a hole and has been in lack
You don't even know how much your leaving made me feel
unwanted

"No one cares," "It's all your fault," are the voices that
continually taunted

You left me empty
So I filled that hole with everything my fingers could touch
You left me empty
So I learned to survive by not letting a good thing out of my
clutch
That same clutch that choked out my first relationship
That same desperate clutch that slowly turned me into an
armored battleship
That same gripping clutch that has kept me hostage in this
dictatorship
That same frantic clutch

Fast forward ten years,
And I'm still figuring out how to survive with my broken
connectors
Unwilling to sell my soul to those pawn shop collectors
Some days I bravely defeat my menacing foes
Other times annihilation is how my story goes
But I've realized that all I can do
Is take life one day at a time

So today, I give myself permission to feel deeply
To respond honestly to this broken planet that I call home
Today, I give myself permission to think critically
To remember that as small as I am, I am never alone
Today, I give myself permission to be messy, healing and to be
fully me

CHAPTER EIGHT

EQUALLY YOKED

Poems about Romantic Partnership

A few months ago, my partner Faithe and I got engaged. The day was perfect! And I'm not just saying that because I am the one who proposed. It was perfect because each moment that I meticulously planned reinforced the singular message that I wanted her to know in the core of her being - I love you forever! So as we giggled our way through the day, all of the joy and elation I felt was contrasted by the last time I had experienced a proposal.

The contours of your heart
Tell a story that would surprise even you

When I was a pastor, my then-boyfriend planned a beautiful night that was meant to go down in history. All of the traditionally approved steps had been taken: we had dated for a few years, he got my family's blessing to get married, and he orchestrated an evening full of thoughtful elements, but as he led me into the final moment, anxiety swept over me. He was everything I was supposed to want - kind, gentle, self-aware and thoughtful, but I had not yet let my mind face the truth that my body was screaming to me: you are gay. If choosing a life partner were based on friendship alone, we could have made it work, but it would have been a union where both of us had to sacrifice critical parts of ourselves. Although so many other people in my life were happy to let me kill my inner voice of knowing in exchange for a traditionally acceptable life, I was hungry for more.

You overwhelm me
In all of the right ways

That relationship highlighted how important it is to have an integrated experience of love. One where our minds, bodies and souls are all invited into full expression. It reminded me that the feelings of attraction, matter. Butterflies and gazes full of wanting, matter. Bodies that vibrate on the same frequency and that are physiologically drawn together, matter.

Your eyes transport me into a world
That is occupied by only us

My relationship is far from perfect but she has shown me the value of finding someone who is interested in seeing, sacrificing, and savoring your partner with an intensity that matches. She has given me the gift of being able to build a life with someone that is anchored by similar values, dreams, and goals. She continually shows up to our relationship with a fierce loyalty and we are able to enjoy the satisfaction of touching another body with a desire that is mirrored. I am blessed to be in an equally yoked partnership where my mind, body, and soul are all engaged.

I want to grow and learn how to love you so deeply
That even your bones can feel it
Lavishing you with affirmation
Working on our communication
To these decisions, I daily commit

I want to practice self-care
And prioritize my own inner-healing
Knowing that a whole me
Knowing that a healthy me
Is the kind of partner you are needing

I want to
I am in this because   want you!

Your *laugh*
Your *eyes*
Your heart and hands
My *care*
My *time*
Your love demands

To say that you are rare and complicated
feels like an oversimplification
To say that I love and need you
feels like an underestimation
To try and speak about your beauty
is to have my native *language fail me*
To try and keep quiet would be
as criminal as threatening to *blackmail me*

So instead, I ask for the strength of this pen to guide me
I breathe in and focus on the growing love inside me

You are lovely, *my dear*
Each curve and line of your face
You are a mystery, *my dear*
The paths to your heart I will trace
You transfix me, *my dear*
Around you all distractions erase
You complete me, *my dear*
I feel whole in your embrace
I love you, *my dear*
Oh I do!

Perfectly intertwined at the heart
Pulsing passion from the start
I get you, you know me
Our connect on happened so naturally
Burning together
Hotter than ever
You are my *twin flame*

Gone are the days of helpless damsels lying around all
distressed and cute
And needing knights and their shiny armour
Instead, strong, driven women are growing up looking for
partners who will help them stay grounded
Not sweep them away into some make-believe fairy tale
These self-aware princesses aren't spending their days gazing
into mirrors to tell them who they are
They have taken the time to unpack baggage,
Set healthy boundaries
And fill their lives with love and positivity
They don't need a person to compliment or complete them
They want a warm-hearted, open-minded, adventurous lover
Who is committed to growth, laughter and listening
They want an equal

Like an unending labyrinth, I get lost in our possibility
Allowing your appeal to pull me deeper into this spiraling maze
In your eyes, I watch our story take shape
Nurtured by your unmoving gaze
Your vision of us feeds me

Your love is juicy, r i c h, nourishment
And my flowers glimmer as I soak in your affection
Walls down and heart finally open
Your love, my only exception

I used to be a *cynic*
Insisting that fate was reserved for
Hollywood and cemeteries

I used to be an *atheist*
Convinced that magic was reserved for
children and fairy tales

I used to be *guarded*
Isolated and keeping everyone at arm's length like
they were all my enemies

I used to be
But you made it your duty
To get close to me
And share your beauty
Now who I used to be
Has been changed by

Your faith

Will you stay and love the parts of me that even I can't; my
skeletons
Will you look at my scars and see my strength, resilience and
determination; my beauty marks
Will you let your eyes adjust to my darkness and bask in my light;
my seasons
Will you love all of me
Will you

Everything was perfect
Sun
Birds
Laughter
You with those brown eyes full of magic and mystery
You with a smile that sent shockwaves into the universe
You with your wild hair flips
You with your lush, full lips
You
All of my senses held captive by your beauty
Eyes feasting
Ears grasping
Heart full

Some people are all about learning the mysteries of outer space
Transfixed by the *grandeur*
Dreaming of life forms from another race
But your eyes call me to move deeper into your inner wild
Mapping, memorizing, musing
Until our lonelys are finally reconciled

To *My Love*,

The universe spoiled me when she gave me the gift of your love
Your affection and relentless support have helped me find
myself and f nally rise above
All the limitations and lies I had subscribed to for years
The way you look at me makes me feel like I can slay dragons
and master all my fears
I know this is going to sound silly, but if I was granted one wish I
would ask the universe to let everyone experience the life-
changing gift of being loved with the kind of loyal and fierce
love you have given me
When I tell you I want to grow my family tree with you
Know that I am picturing
My roots plunging deep into your fountain
Soaking up your life-giving sap
I am
Connected, committed, and captivated by you
I will
Cherish, nurture and fight for you
I love you always
In all ways

CHAPTER NINE

SELF REGENERATION

Poems about Comfort + Regulation

Comfort is what we crave after our attachment wounds have been activated. When a word or action sets off the invisible trip wires that trauma has installed in our bodies, we stop accessing logic and reason and are launched into our fight-or-flight mode. As we are comforted, our aggravated souls drink deeply of the validation and safety that she brings. Comfort is the cleansing ointment that slowly heals us from the harmful impacts of surviving the darkness of our world's shadow side.

Comfort is a healing salve
That should be applied
Liberally

For so long, I didn't know how to ingest comfort unless it came from an external source. I somehow knew it was what I needed, and I greedily drank up every supply I could get my hands on, but didn't yet know how to cultivate my own stream of it. So I found comfort in the noisiness of a packed social calendar and in the validation of humanitarian work. I found it in substances and sweaty bodies. In the moody solidarity of a worship song's minor chords. In the predictable safety of a partner's embrace or the melodic tempo of a rushing river. I am so thankful for the soothing impact of nature, people, and art, as they have anchored my body, but learning how to stabilize my mind-body connection from the inside out has accelerated the transformation of my trauma into fertilizer.

I'm practicing the art
Of self-healing

Lately, I have been learning how to comfort myself. How to hold, and gently care for, my precious yet tender feelings. How to lovingly soothe and sit with my inner child as I parent her into wholeness. This practice is changing my life. This practice is healing me. It means that I no longer have to depend on external sources to be available 24/7 to sustain me - I can ground and regulate myself anytime I need it. I can tap into the medicine of the breath to reverse inflammation and infection. I can seek refuge in the strength and support of my own caresses. I can get lost in the compassion vibrating from my own eyes. Comforting myself means that I can satisfy my own thirsts from the deep reservoirs of living water that spring up from within me.

My feelings will not overwhelm me
I can feel hard things

My feelings are clues and teachers
Pointing me toward truth and discovery

My feelings don't always tell the full story
But their existence needs validation

My feelings are energy
So I will let them flow through me

My feelings are part of me
So they will be considered and cared for as I parent them
with love

You think it's weak
When I tenderly caress my body
And hold space for her to metabolize my anger into tears
But I am light and free and joyful
And I've been able to confront my darkness
And reframe my fears

You think it's a waste of time
To give voice to my rage and shame
And disappointment and strife
But my heart has been validated
And the return on investment she offers
Is wholeness as I journey through life

I will run
And cry
And grieve
And heal
Over, and over again

Until I am able to stop running from the present
Until I no longer cry over memories immortalized in the past
Until I can stop grieving the potential of our future
Until my lungs can in-take air without aching
Until the sheets of my bed wrapping around me, stop
comforting me like your embrace used to
Until I heal

I look you square in the eyes and tell you to leave
And then spend the next 3 hours wishing you were here to nurse
my loneliness

-Need

Like a sacred ceremony, I
p
  o
    u
      r
My *grief, weariness,* and *pain*
Into these pen and paper containers
And watch as new life emerges
Like hidden treasures
Sifted out by strainers

Time did what time always does
It *taunted* me
It *tortured* me
It *taught* me
It dragged me to the edge of desperation
And then, it gently carried me back
Time did what you chose not to do
It kept on showing up

My senses are on high alert
As potent extractions of my inner world erupt to the surface
My deep calls out
How can so much sadness and excitement simultaneously
coexist?
How can both fear and security rule my heart?
Logic and reason conquered by emotions venom
So I root myself in my own embodied awareness and create a
sanctuary w thin
I am both
Anchored and free
As the waves and breakers of this waterfall
Roll over me

I am not afraid of these tears that cleanse us
They wash away the jealousy and areas that collected dust

I am not afraid of this void that your leaving made
For it's a deep enough hole for a new foundation to be laid

I am not afraid of the space that we agreed to take
For room is sometimes all that is needed for a life to remake

I am not afraid

I do the hard work of
Sifting and sitting
In the ache of my feelings
So that I can show up
And be seen by

Y o u

Feeling nothing has its perks
No heartache
No shattered expectations
Whatever the outcome, it works
'You want to leave', okay, sweet!
'You're seeing someone new', when can we all meet?

Feeling nothing has its advantages
No devastation
No unexpected depression
No gaping wounds in need of bandages
'You've been lying this whole time', no big deal
'You're no longer in love', isn't that how we all feel

But feeling nothing, leaves you feeling like nothing

Hold me
Comfort me
Tell me these demons can be prayed away

See me
Learn me
Empathize with these raging anxieties

Validate me
Affirm me
Our connection anchors me through this storm

I'm sorry
Teach me
You matter
I'm listening
I need you

CHAPTER TEN

A SEXUAL RE-EDUCATION

Poems about Sex

The mantra, "Save yourself until marriage" was ingrained into my psyche as a teenager and characterized all my sexual conduct deep into my adult life. The shame-based sexual education the Church handed me through the purity culture movement forbade any curiosity or conversation around sexual pleasure and demanded complete physical mastery. Once, I tearfully confessed to masturbating to my pastor and was told that if God had truly delivered me from that temptation, I needed to publicly confess my "sin" to my youth congregation and give God glory for saving me from the demons of lust. The idea that women were deemed desirable as long as their innocence and virginity were intact left me feeling weary and uninspired sexually.

Sex is healing

Leaving the church presented a beautiful, and necessary opportunity to begin my sexual re-education. For the first time, I was able to explore what I wanted, needed, and desired in safe, and consensual spaces. I learned to cherish every melanated curve of my body and recognize the value of energetic exchanges. I taught myself to release the mental and emotional chains that held me captive to the hetero-normative ideal of sex and lean into the beauty and glitter of my queer experience. Indulging in the liberatory principles discussed in Pleasure Activism by Adrienne Marie Brown and The Vagina Bible by Dr. Jen Gunther helped dismantle the pillars of misinformation I had erected about the magical workings of the human body.

My pussy is your kingdom
And you rule her well

My approach to sexuality is now more fluid and flexible. My partner Faithe has played an instrumental role in establishing a playful prioritization of pleasure in my life. Her sexy confidence and love for the erotic has modelled how our primal passions can be harnessed and heightened when shame and fear are removed from the bedroom. Surrendering to the ecstasy of sexual relationships has been a powerful tool for connection and comfort. Within her wild, I have allowed myself to become untamed. After years of keeping my sexual desires on a tight leash and starving her appetites, I have finally been freed up to crave and connect; to climax and cum. And for that, I am eternally grateful.

Sex is communication
Our limbs tell a story through each intimate vibration
Wordless exploration
Breathless intoxication

Sex is communication
So come and share with me

You are the goddess of fire
Sparking
Lighting
Causing me to burn with desire

You are the ambassador of pleasure
Pulling
Stirring
The source of ecstasy without measure

You are the master seduction
Pulsing
Dripping
Taking me to the place of final eruption

You are, so have me

I am always *jealous*

I am *jealous* of your sheets
how they are able to hold you every night
I am *jealous* of the rain
how it so tenderly glides over your skin
For the spoon that you so easily let enter your mouth
For the oxygen that has free access to your most intimate parts

Baby, I am always *jealous*

Your wild force
Your seductive frame
Sweat and passion defining our pulsing rhythm
As I breathlessly whisper your name
Our hunger matches
Our addiction, the same
I am your willing possession
Gladly consumed by your flame

You let me enter your arms and like sand that sinks
I'm buried
My hands explore your winding curves and like water that flows
We're carried
Your lips push slowly
Your hips thrust toward me
Your scent and taste mix to create an intoxicating potion
I drink deep as you lovingly pour out your devotion

I want you
It's simple
It's clear
It's true

I need you
It's consuming
It's strong
It's you

My body drapes itself around you
Complimenting your curves like a perfectly tailored garment
The softness of your skin
An ancient formula replicated by only the lushest flowers
So like a wave consuming the shore
I swallow you whole

The brushes and strokes
Of your whispering evokes
A kind of tingling that stokes
This fire for you

Your body *t r a n s p o r t s* me
into a world
that is occupied
by only us

Steam fogs the mirror
Water and wanting m ngle
Bathing made holy

CHAPTER ELEVEN

RAINBOWS IN THE DARK

Poems about Queerness

I was in fourth grade when I had my first crush on a female. While all my friends were fawning over boys, I was starry-eyed for one of my close girlfriends. I was eager for every opportunity to be in her presence and uninhibited in my affectionate adoration for her. Not having adequate tools for self-discovery, I eventually chalked it up to a desire to be best friends. Later on, my Christian conditioning taught me that this part of myself was something I had to reject and change. Visions of brimstone and hellfire were preached from the pulpit so often that I refused to admit my queerness even to myself. Instead, I leaned into my spiritual calling, embarked on my pastoral journey and internalized deep, harmful shame. It took twenty-seven years to admit my queerness and another three before I was able to live into this beautiful intersection proudly.

Your binary was not meant to be contained

I now see that my queerness is a gift. The diversity of our expression as a community has invited me to explore the spectrum of sexuality without being boxed in by permanent labels. The marginalization of this identity has increased my capacity for empathy and strengthened my resilience. Living in Toronto has gifted me the privileged opportunity to publicly embrace my queerness in a city that has a vibrant and established community. Although as a country we have work to do around LGBTQ2+ inclusion, Toronto is a beautiful pocket of openness and diversity with a great selection of queer leagues, events, and collectives; opportunities for affinity and connection are plentiful.

Queer (cuue-earr): The by-product of glitter and magic making love

In spite of all the hardships and hurdles, coming out has been one of the most rewarding adventures of my life. Choosing who to love should not be a communal decision, so embrace your rainbow and live into your queerness fully because I can promise you it will be worth it. For you were created with a tender elegance and an unforgettable beauty. Your glittering curves were forged in the fires of lonely discovery. Cosmic hands were commissioned to design the deep wells of diversity that define your attractions. Your tender heart and fierce strides inspire movements of liberation. All of the swirls and shapes of your embodied expression are needed and celebrated. Your essence is timeless. Your presence is fragrant. You are magic and mystery perfected!

We exist

We are fabulous queens with fros and feathers

We are smooth-talking studs packing more swag than a traveler's bulging suitcase

We are bootylicious bosses with braids and beat faces

We defy oppression in our dance, celebration and joy

This is our space

We have claimed it so that we can take lots of it up

Our bodies belong here

Our expression is needed here

Our pleasure is our protest

I never had the words for how you made me feel
And yet, every dormant, repressed cell in my body
Knew how to respond to your nearness
No label was needed

I never had the language for how we clicked and flowed
And yet, every loving glance we shared
Made me want to twirl, hide and giggle all at the same time
No moment was wasted

So I gave you the most honoured title I knew
You were my Best Friend

Wouldn't it be nice

To not have to strategically plan
And emotionally prepare
To simply leave your house
because the way you presented didn't make others stare
To not have to think twice
about publicly holding your lover's hand
For fear of danger or the homophobic slurs
that you might have to withstand

Wouldn't it be nice

Playful glances
Holding hands
Late-night snuggles
Weekend plans
Chemistry bubbling
Signals green
Best friends and lovers
Is this a dream

Oh, you're straight

I did everything I could
To see those beautiful lips of yours break into a smile
To learn every curious corner of your mind
To have the intensity of your gaze rest on me
To show you that I was just as invested
To make you feel safe and seen

I never had the words
So I let my body do the talking

You can't ignore us if we refuse to go away
You can't dismiss our needs if we expose the systems you use to
bury them
You can't other us if we will not stay separate

We will continue to show up in our skin and take up lots of
space
As these margins are made central

My design
Divided by
Your attract on
Is the sum tctal
Of this heartbreak

Was it that I never had the words?
Or were they scrubbed from my mind?
Shame poured over my bcdy like bleach
Bleach, designed to break up my molecular composition and
remove all colour
Shame, designed to dilute my rainbow and erode all of my
tender fleshy bits
Was it that I never had the words?
Or were they scrubbed from my mind?

You try to shrink my identities to fit your neatly labelled boxes
Policing my body
Mocking my pride
You say that I am welcome at your table
And then take offence when I refuse to drink your cup of shame
But I am long familiar with the empty promises and potent
poisons that chalice holds
I know the bitter aftertaste of her intoxication
And I am not interested
You try to shrink my identities
But it only makes you look small

I've always been told that love will show up wearing either blue or pink
Requiring one of each colour for there to be a true link
But as I look around my city, I love the colour fusions that surround me
Shades and hues mixing and creating new colours that can be primary
So I will keep on resisting anyone who tries to limit my expression of love
Letting rainbows remind them that my attraction is painted in the heavens above

Dear Dad,

They told me that it's your fault that I'm gay
That if the younger me had gotten more love and affirmation
I wouldn't have turned out this way
There should have been fewer rules and lots of play
More of you and mommy kissing
That would have kept the gay away

But if this formula was true
Then I know lots of straight people that should have my story today
And lots of gay people who have loving families
But proudly wear their rainbows on display

Dad, even though my childhood wasn't perfect
Thank you for nourishing me with your love in the present day

Locked behind your eyes I see
Dreams of a love that can never be
These irregular hearts were never meant to fit
Our divided attraction is a truth that we can't remit

My vibrant inner colours seep through the thin layer of flesh that veil them

These days I am memorizing the chants that say my difference is a rare gem

Ignoring the cynics that try to make you conform or they condemn

Besides, in what world are rainbows and unicorns scary?

CHAPTER TWELVE

SEASONS

Poems about Loss + Change

When I was twelve, my fifteen-year-old brother died from cancer. After years of my family hoping, praying, and trying anything to secure his recovery, I lost my protector, basketball coach, and built-in best friend. Overnight the familiar din of chaos was replaced with empty silence and the cold reality that nothing lasts forever. This was the first time I tasted the bitter nectar of loss and learned that grief is not linear. Life, like loss, has an assortment of seasons. Every time I consider the bareness of nature during winter, I am reminded that death is part of life. If we will allow the healing qualities of time to germinate, new life always stirs within the darkness of our loss. In the end, there is so much we can glean from accepting the inevitability of seasons.

The fleeting beauty of creation
Reminds me that our flourishing is part of our purpose

Seasons remind us of life's impermanence. They remind us that we are on a fleeting, temporal journey through this reality. Just like the beauty of a flower explodes into the present and then wilts away, our glory also has an expiry date. We are here one day and gone the next. Taking in life from our human vantage point one day and returning to the ground that supports all of life the next. Making choices that reinforce joy, growth, and adventure are top priorities. Our impermanence reminds us that we are all a unique combination of each other - recycled particles, energy, and stardust. It is an invitation to care for each other and the land with the same level of respect and consideration we would hold for ourselves.

We cling to the security and comfort of forever
When so much of life is meant to be lived out in seasons

Seasons invite us into the beauty of the present. Each season is alive with its own set of unique blessings and lessons. If we don't live in the moment, we miss taking in the awe-inspiring beauty that life on this planet has to offer. I love the way my neighbours' unique gardens summon me to slow down and see the beauty of the present. Rushing through life causes us to miss out on the trove of treasures right in front of our eyes. What happens beyond the gift of this moment is out of our control. For there is a time for all things, an invitation from life to feel and experience all of the diversity and adventure she has to offer. All of life's living happens when we are present with ourselves, nature, and each other.

Starting new chapters is uncomfortable
Because they are littered with challenge and change

Seasons invite us to practice surrender. They remind us that there is a gift wrapped up in the energy of trust. The flowers don't spend their days stressed, instead they bloom boldly. Similarly, we have not been called to worry about anything, but we burn up so much creative energy dwelling on what-ifs and worst-case scenarios. I am all about authoring the lives we want, but once we have done all that we can do, it is advantageous for us to step into gratitude and trust that the universe is for us. That doesn't mean that transitioning into a new season isn't tricky. I struggle with being honest with myself and letting places, people, and positions fall away like shedding leaves. Even still, learning to recognize the signs of shifting seasons is a life skill that witnessing nature is helping me foster.

In our dying, we are healed

Detox your life now
Join the trees in shedding the toxins, judgment and shame
Let those mindsets that aren't serving you wilt and fall away
Those energies that are stunting you
Those dreams that are too small
Let them all die

Because in our dying we are healed

You etched my flowers onto your skin
So they would never wilt
Ensuring that they would be immune to changing seasons
Stormproof
You took a part of me inside yourself
Permanently uniting features that define us
Cross-pollination
You wore me proudly
Letting me stand out as black on skin always does
But the reality of our adventure is that it always had a time
stamp
And the truth about my petals is that they were never meant to
be forever

Hibernating hopes thaw
As the long months of darkness and isolation
Metamorphosize into budding blossoms of colour, creativity and connection
My bones feel the shift
Lapping up the lingering light that looms longer and longer on my doorstep

- *Spring*

I know that at one point, you were madly in love with me
I watched you tirelessly fight for our success
I watched you bury your heart inside my chest
Watering it continually with your sweat and devotion
But your interest has waned
Your vision has grown dull
Your heart is now scattered among many fields
Do I wait
Believing that one day the fire will return to your eyes
Or do I thank the gods for your love
And let you go

I don't regret loving you
The flames of our un on have both warmed and seared me

I don't regret needing you
The depth of our connection has both rooted and freed me

I don't regret learning you
The paths of your heart have both awed and challenged me

Just know, I don't regret a single moment

I tasked you with the simple job of fixing me
Entered this relationship and unloaded all my expectations on
you gently
Make me happy
Make me whole
Love my baggage
Feed my soul

Weary from this task, I watch you leave

I am in the process of retraining my toes
Feet used to taking strides toward you
Now betray me with their instincts
So accustomed to the rhythm of your strides
Now walking away

You loved how I would let myself break just to get your
attention
That everything in my life was a disaster, except for you
You needed me to need your neediness
I believed your lies because no one told me I didn't have to
I let you demand, demean, and then dispose of me
But
I have glimpsed my reflection in the chains you designed to
cage me
And I saw glory contained.
You threw me in this dungeon expecting me to rot
But
My roots are starting to reach deep enough to sustain
nourishment
My voice strong enough to start attracting attention
My wings are emerging and I am not afraid to take the leap
I reject your poison and I see through your sorcery
I cancel your darkness and harm with each deliberate step
forward
With my growth.

Not the darkness of the *tomb*
But the darkness of the *womb*
New life emerging
As I blossom and *bloom*

CHAPTER THIRTEEN

LIBERATED AND EMPOWERED

Poetic Affirmations

A number of traumatic experiences from my childhood left me feeling helpless and vulnerable to the big bad monster called life. Tragic moments would roll in, shatter everything that was safe and familiar, and leave me feeling powerless. So I spent years taking a backseat to my own story.

I am competent and capable

The problem is that those energy patterns followed me into my adult life and began to rob me of my voice and confidence. Even though I was not a helpless child anymore, I continued to default to the familiar posture of the victim. I silently allowed others to tell me how they saw me and what I was capable of, even when their limited assessments caged my infinite potential. Although creating healthy boundaries was something I was working on, being optimistic and positive was second nature for me. So when I started to spiral into a dark depression, I knew I needed a serious change.

I am strong and secure

After days of laying in my bed I decided that if I can't give myself the pep-talk that I needed, I would recruit songs and affirmations to support me. I created my "Daily Affirmations" playlist and added any track that felt motivational and empowering to it. I started leaving notes around my condo and promised myself to read them out loud every time I saw them. The potency of habit fused with the regenerative power that lives within each spoken word began to transmute my mental toxins into treasures. My perception of self and ability to navigate life shifted as I preached truth over my soul. The more I watched the growth take shape right before my eyes, the more obsessed I became with the art of spelling. I began writing nutrient-rich affirmations that I ingested daily like a vitamin.

I found the keys to liberation

Now when ill-fitting and outdated thoughts and beliefs creep in, I intentionally speak a new empowered reality over my soul. I am learning to trust the voice of love to lead me through every dark valley. I am learning how to speak to every barren part of my being and command life knowing that each word is a seed that returns a harvest.

Thoughts, breath and vision intermingle to produce words
Every spoken syllable sprouting and whirling into action
They work to accomplish their assignment:
Life, hope, death, division

You choose

I will dream a new way
I will be a new way
I will transport tomorrow's radical imaginings into the work of today
I will imperfectly live into my values
I will value the life tangled up in my imperfections
I will measure all of my organizing and pushing and growing with the cords of love
Which means, I will allow self-compassion and patience, and generosity to support and sustain all of my organizing and pushing, and growing

"No one is going to show up for me"
"No one is going to care"
These are old narratives that I will longer share

"I am worthy of connection"
"I am deserving of love"
These are transformational gifts that I will lavishly partake of

nothing thrives under a critical gaze
so
fill your glances with affection that splash over her like the
morning dew
let the lavish tumblings of your adoration drench every part of
her being

nothing thrives under a critical gaze
so
nourish her with the strength of your truthful, tender affirmation
flood her heart with detailed visions of her greatness

and then
watch her flourish

Did you know
That you are the universe incarnate
Her magnitude and splendor clothed in flesh and feeling
You have her mind - it's expansive and captivating
You have her eyes - full of substance and mercy
You have her heart - so courageous and tender
I look at you, and I see the same vibrancy that I adore so much
in her
Every time you embody joy, resilience and creativity
You look just like her

So when I say, you have all you need for this moment
It's because I know she has given it to you,
It's because I know it's already in you
All of the power, creativity, energy and resource that you need
for your next big thing
Is yours
So may you sit-in and soak-up and be saturated-by this truth
May you allow your eyes to behold and your heart to take it
May you step into your power with confidence and assurance

Joy is my i n h e r i t a n c e
Lightness, laughter and a deeply rooted knowing of my
unchanging belovedness
Are my i n h e r i t a n c e

When you say " I am" you are extending a universal invitation
A key that gives access to higher-power for their participation
Belief and energy united, creating a solid foundation
So what life are you building with each "I am" affirmation?

I am magic and mystery
I am darkness and wonder
I am never stuck
I am deserving of my own forgiveness
I am an unsolved puzzle
I am beautifully broken
I am perfectly imperfect

You are stardust in drag
Costumed
Covered
Concealed

You are a princess under a bag
Refined
Royal
Righteous

You are the object of the universes brag
Mesmerizing
Moving
Majestic

You are
So just be

YOU are all YOU have been waiting for
Stop substituting yourself for over-processed look-alikes
Stop shrinking and holding back
Stop doubting and accepting lack
Show up and shine

I believe in you
I see you as you really are
I know you can do anything

But all the faith I have in you
Will never make up
For the lack of your own

Because lasting change
Needs to emerge from the inside
It needs to start at home

Bigger
Bolder
R o o m to breathe
R o o m to grow
R o o m to discover
R o o m to be wrong
R o o m
This space once bulging with your excess is now mine
I'm no longer suffocated; roots pushing against walls
I'm no longer smothered; lungs gasping underwater
I'm no longer confined

I am innately rooted
And deeply connected
To the same power
That created the universe

Growth is a characteristic of things that are living:
Sprouting, wilting
Pruning, changing
Taking and giving

Growth is an option when life presents you with change:
Intentional, deliberate
Not by accident
Own and rearrange

Growth is the treasure desired throughout the journey,
So throughout the journey, treasure the desire for growth

CHAPTER FOURTEEN

LOVE IS OUR BIRTHRIGHT

Poems about Self-Love + Connection

I 've lived long enough on this planet to know that what my partner Faithe and I share is rare and extremely valuable. She is my soulmate, lover, and my number-one favorite gift from the Universe. The depth of knowing and history that we have been able to cultivate over the 15-plus years of friendship and eventual partnership means that she has been able to reflect back to me honest depictions of my heart. The slow undressing of our masks and make-up has been the most intimate and freeing exchange of my life. When I couldn't see the courage smoldering under the piles of ash that surrounded me, she directed my eyes to their flickering light. When I felt washed out and depleted, she increased the brightness all around me so that I could see the vibrant bold colours that flushed my form. Her love has done what love always does. It has healed me and made me more.

Love looks like something

Love is wrapped up in the gift of our presence. In the energy that accompanies our attention. It's in the warm and tender touches.

Love is choosing not to run when someone lets you see their human, their ugly. It's commitment that can be touched, tasted, and seen. It's having someone who can both call you out and compliment you with the same level of precision. Love is long and steady. Love is slow and deep. It's letting someone else have the "win." It doesn't need to parade itself all over town, but it is unmistakable when it is in the room.

Love can be cultivated anywhere

But love is not just one thing, love is all things. Love does not have one face; rather, it is etched onto the canvas of all faces. It is meant to be both savored and shared - ingested and emitted. Love asks us to treat every soul with respect and dignity. It invites us to lean into an energy that fosters mutual flourishing. Love asks us to drain the poisons of fear and scarcity out of our beings, so that we can transcend those emotional handicaps and start cultivating the fruits of loving-kindness in our world. Love deserves to be enjoyed by everyone.

Love is a mysterious and mighty force

So the next time you go through a dry season and the signs of love are hard to find, I invite you to go outside and let nature whisper her love songs over your soul. Let the gradual sprouting of the oak tree remind you that not everything is instant - life unfolds in seasons. Let the newness of each sunrise remind you that your story is not over - let it be your fresh canvas. I invite you to go inside and paint the walls of your mind with images of peace and comfort. I invite you to be the love that you are looking for and watch those seeds of kindness sprout and bear fruit. I invite you to claim it - for love is your birthright!

In seasons of dancing and disappointment
She stuck by me
She saw me and never looked away
She saw me and wanted more

The pride and tenderness emitting from her gaze
Slowly cleared the dirt that distorted my features
Her words cast spells over my world
She lathered my head with life and power

So I began to step into their promise
The truth of her love
Set me free

Thank you for sitting with me
And giving me the gift of your nearness
I love that you always make room for my tears

You have shown me the kind of support and confidence
That I needed to finally let go of those small beliefs
The ones that had me constantly shrinking myself to fit their
molds

You tilted my chin up and taught me how to dream again
Cultivating an atmosphere ripe with healing potential
You led the way and showed me how to create new life

And like a mother, love softly whispers into my hair,
"*Greater things are yet to come my child.*
Don't you know that you will never walk alone."

Cease striving and just be
Trust me you are enough
I'll keep writing these love notes
Till you are rooted in their reality
And your edges are no longer rough

Stay soft
Stay vulnercble
Stay true
Embrace the mess clong with the beauty
For in the mess beauty always shine through

As we slow down to feel and hold each other's stories
This dream, it grows and expands
So let's take time to curiously explore our identities and
differences
For this is what *truly* loving each other demands

Our collective healing and humanity are interconnected
Which means: we thrive and fall together
So let's leave behind the comfort of ease and excuse
And let hope be our unifying tether

Lasting change happens when
We stop resisting
And dreading
And running from
And fighting against
And fixating on
The pain

When we can zoom out and see the full picture
Not just the hard parts
Or how much it will cost us

Lasting change happens as we stare the emptiness of insanity
in the eyes
And finally see that we deserve better
That it is time to evolve
And shed skin
And change
That is the moment you know
This time will be different

You heal me as you teach me the language of connection
Letting your honesty and courage pour over me like affection
Disclosing tragedies, failures and your hearts dearest lessons
Inviting truth when you ask me, "How are you," and not being
shocked by my confessions

We laugh late into the night
Sharing dreams
Exchanging stories
You ask about my childhood
I hold your scars carefully
I leave feeling seen and supported

-Friendship

Thank you for time
Thank you for the gift of age
Each sun cycle brimming with guidance
As you lead us with the wisdom of a sage

Lessons on flourishing
Bud and blossom all around me
Patiently anchoring my soul
Like the rooting of an ancient tree

CHAPTER FIFTEEN

UNTIL NEXT TIME

Our Promise Land Poem

Coming to the end of writing this book feels bittersweet. A part of me is excited to get my life back because working on this project has required so much of my free time. The other truth is that I have loved being the person who spends their days writing poems of gratitude to the land and creating space for my body to share her stories. I have grown from sitting with the honest parts of my soul and not letting their rawness be edited away. Writing this book has been an exercise in showing up for my dreams and nurturing my own integrity.

You can author the life you want

If I can leave you with one truth that was reinforced for me during this season, it would be to never stop investing in the cultivation of your inner world. Our thoughts, feelings, and beliefs all work together to create our reality. The gifts of stillness, community, gratitude, and education help root us in truth and keep our default scripts updated. Life is one big invitation to shine and shed, to bury and bloom. So continue to nurture the garden of your soul and watch it produce blessings and breakthroughs. Your flourishing is worth the energy and effort it takes for you to show up for yourself. Your dreams, expression, and impact are uniquely yours and they matter. In the end, I hope your experience of 'Homecoming' has been both a gift and a road map home.

Our Promise Land - *A Spoken Word Poem*

Let me sing you the story of our milk and honey
Where rivers are lush and brimming
It's the song of our collective tomorrow
Where our lights are bright and not dimming
It's a tale of inclusion and glory
Where all are one and hopes are new
Let me sing you the story of our milk and honey
Until it becomes your story too

It was exactly what we were promised
And, it was so much more
The rivers teemed with life as truth flowed through them
Her soil was rich with the medicine of loving kindness
But the part that I can't stop thinking about
The part that still gives me the most hope
Was seeing the liberated youth who embodied their truth
Using their voices and vision for good
It was seeing how power-sharing and community caring
Could bring dignity and humanity into every neighborhood
I have tasted the fruits of her promise
And I say, our creator can be trusted, so

Let me sing you the story of our milk and honey
Where rivers are lush and brimming
It's the song of our collective tomorrow
Where our lights are bright and not dimming
It's a tale of inclusion and glory
Where all are one and hopes are new
Let me sing you the story of our milk and honey
Until it becomes your story too

I've been there, I know it

I've tasted and I've seen
So let's build the change
And be the change
Because, I too have a dream
I said
I've been there, I know it
I've tasted and I've seen
So let's build the change
And be the change
Because, I too have a dream

The dream is in this song of milk and honey
Where rivers are lush and brimming
It's in the hope of our collective tomorrow
Where our lights are bright and not dimming
The dream spills out of these tales of inclusion and glory
Where all are one and hopes are new
So I say, let's live into our promise of milk and honey

I'm going there, how about you?

ABOUT THE AUTHOR

Heather is a tea-drinking, female-loving, ex-evangelical pastor turned poet and facilitator. In her work, she prioritizes resourcing communities with tools for rebuilding, reimagining, and reconciling differences through art and storytelling.

Heather is committed to creating content birthed out of her queer, black and indigenous identities. She envisions a world where systemic change is fueled by our individual and collective liberation - a world where all people have equitable access to holistic healing through art, education, and authentic connections.

You can catch her speaking to a wide range of audiences, notably churches, conferences, universities, and art shows. To follow her journey and view her work, connect on Instagram at @heatsbeam or her website: *heatherbeamish.com*

Manufactured by Amazon.ca
Bolton, ON